INDIA

Susie Brooks

The LAND and the PEOPLE

Published in paperback in 2017 by Wayland

Editor: Nicola Edwards
Design: Dave Ball and Angela Ball at D&A
Cover design: D&A
Map artist: Stefan Chabluk

ISBN: 978 0 7502 9809 4
10 9 8 7 6 5 4 3 2 1

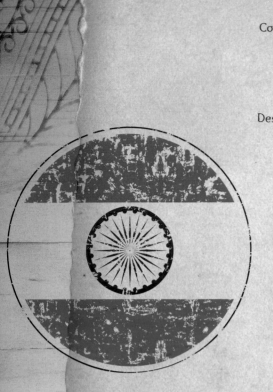

MIX
Paper from
responsible sources
FSC
www.fsc.org
FSC® C104740

Wayland, an imprint of
Hachette Children's Group
Part of Hodder and Stoughton
Carmelite House
50 Victoria Embankment
London EC4Y 0DZ

An Hachette UK Company
www.hachette.co.uk
www.hachettechildrens.co.uk

Printed in Singapore

Picture acknowledgements: All images and graphic elements courtesy of Shutterstock except p12 (l) Wikimedia Commons; p13 (b) Wikimedia Commons; p21 (tl) Corbis; p26 Corbis; p28 (b) Alamy; p29 (t) Alamy; p30 Alamy; p33 Corbis; p40 Corbis; p41 (r) Corbis; p44 Corbis

The website addresses (URLs) included in this book were valid at the time of going to press. However, it is possible that contents or addresses may have changed since the publication of this book. No responsibility for any such changes can be accepted by either the author or the Publisher.

CONTENTS

INDIA ON THE MAP

PAKISTAN

It is hard not to notice India! It's the largest country in southern Asia and has the second-biggest population on the planet. Developing super-fast and bursting with exciting customs, this is a place that really makes its mark on the world.

New Delhi

INDIA

MORE THAN ONE HUNDRED LANGUAGES ARE SPOKEN IN INDIA AND EACH STATE HAS ITS OWN OFFICICAL LANGUAGE.

India fact file

Population: 1,251,695,584 (July 2015 est.)

Area (land and sea): 3,287,263 sq km

Capital city: New Delhi

Highest peak: Kanchenjunga (8,585m)

Main language: Hindi

Currency: Indian rupee

CHINA

NEPAL

BHUTAN

BANGLADESH

MYANMAR

SRI
LANKA

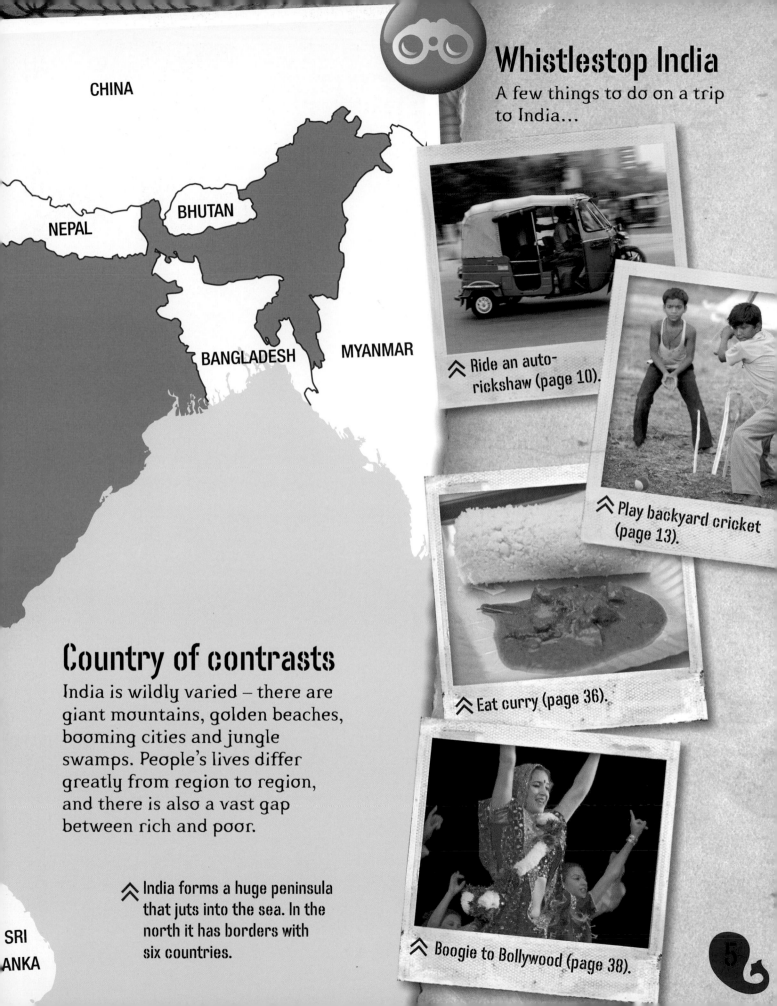

⚠ Ride an auto-
rickshaw (page 10).

⚠ Play backyard cricket
(page 13).

⚠ Eat curry (page 36).

⚠ Boogie to Bollywood (page 38).

Country of contrasts
India is wildly varied – there are
giant mountains, golden beaches,
booming cities and jungle
swamps. People's lives differ
greatly from region to region,
and there is also a vast gap
between rich and poor.

⚠ India forms a huge peninsula
that juts into the sea. In the
north it has borders with
six countries.

A BILLION AND BEYOND

India's population has rocketed past the billion mark, making it home to one in seven people on Earth! The story began more than 5,000 years ago, with one of the world's oldest civilisations...

The Mughal Emperor Humayun was buried here.

INDIA'S INFLLUENCE HAS TRICKLED INTO MANY ASPECTS OF OUR CULTURE, FROM FOOD TO TECHNOLOGY TO WORDS LIKE PYJAMAS, SHAMPOO AND BUNGALOW!

Ancient India

Way back in 3,000BCE, cities were growing up in the Indus Valley (above), the region that gave India its name. The people that lived here built great fortresses and developed many advanced systems, from sewers and drains to writing, weights and trade. Buttons, flush toilets and rulers all originated in ancient India!

India is expected to be the most populous country in the world by 2035.

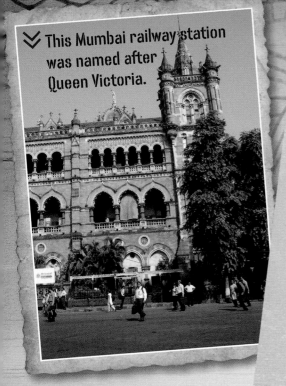

⌄ This Mumbai railway station was named after Queen Victoria.

✓ INDEPENDENT INDIA

India broke free from British rule in 1947, but there were conflicts within the country. Muslim areas were divided off to form what are now Pakistan and Bangladesh, while India kept a Hindu majority. A million people died in riots or on arduous journeys to find new homes. There are still tensions in some regions today, especially the disputed territory of Kashmir between India and Pakistan. But most people in India live in harmony, with many religions and over 100 languages between them.

Foreign powers

Over the centuries, various foreign powers invaded India. By 1526, most of the country was ruled by Muslim Mughals from central Asia. In the 1700s, the British East India Company (a trading firm) began to take over and in 1858, India became a part of the British Empire.

⌃ Daily flag-lowering ceremony on India's border with Pakistan

Famous Indians

Amitabh Bachchan – a big-name star in India's film industry

Mahatma Gandhi – led the campaign for Indian independence

Mother Teresa – dedicated her life to helping the poor

Sachin Tendulkar – hailed as one of the best cricketers of all time

MEET THE MEGACITIES

Only a third of all Indians live in urban areas – even so, this chockablock country has three megacities! Delhi, Mumbai and Kolkata are all home to over 10 million people, and many other cities are creeping close to this mark.

>> Mumbai lies on the west coast of India and is home to the country's busiest port.

Big Delhi

Delhi is India's capital city, with close to 25 million inhabitants. The government is based in New Delhi's elegant buildings, while the old town centres around the Mughal Red Fort. All the colours and cultures of India are crammed into Delhi's hectic streets. Crossing the road or wiggling through a crowded market can be a challenge!

≪ It's easy to see how the Red Fort got its name!

≪ New Delhi's great buildings were designed by British architects in the early twentieth century.

Mega Mumbai

When it comes to business and finance, Mumbai is India's hub. A seething city of over 20 million people, its industries include banking, engineering, textiles, food processing and diamond polishing. The suburban railway here carries more than 7.5 million commuters a day!

Mumbai's famous dhoti ghat, the world's largest outdoor laundry.

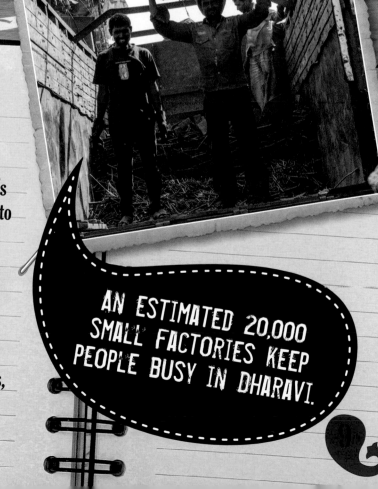

FOCUS ON

☑ **SLUM SETTLERS**

Migrants from the countryside stream into India's cities all the time, hoping to find jobs but unable to afford decent housing. This has led to the spread of shanty towns or slums, where rents are low but living conditions are poor. In central Mumbai, Dharavi is a slum of over a million people — it's overcrowded and homes are makeshift, but there is still a thriving community. Residents make their living through a mind-blowing range of enterprises, from recycling (right) to guided tours.

AN ESTIMATED 20,000 SMALL FACTORIES KEEP PEOPLE BUSY IN DHARAVI.

I t can feel like rush hour all day long when you're travelling in India! The biggest crowds pile onto trains, buses and other road vehicles, though there are flights between most major cities.

≪ An autorickshaw, or tuk-tuk, is a nifty way to get around town.

City streets

Many people in India own cars or motorbikes, but public transport is usually jam-packed. Look out for small, open-sided tuk-tuks (so-called because of the noise they make), dodging through the streets with their horns tooting. Usually it's the biggest vehicles that get the right of way, though!

≪ India's cities, such as Mumbai, shown here, are affected by pollution from noisy, chaotic traffic.

Creative travel

'Full' doesn't mean much in India! People will cling to the back of buses, pile onto jeep roofs or balance a whole family on a motorcycle if they're short of a seat. Walking is a popular way to get around too – not to mention an ox-cart, elephant or camel ride.

>> More Indians own motorbikes than cars.

>> A train takes a scenic route in Goa, western India.

VEHICLES SHARE THE ROAD WITH COWS, WHICH ARE SACRED TO HINDUS AND TEND TO WANDER WHERE THEY LIKE.

⌃ Cows can be a hazard, but they're free to roam the roads.

FOCUS ON

☑ **INDIAN RAIL**

India's rail network is one of the world's busiest and could wrap around the equator 1.5 times. More than 11,000 trains run a day, employing about 1.4 million people. Some carriages are luxurious, while in others passengers pile onto multi-storey bunks or wooden benches. Chai sellers and other vendors hop on and off at over 6,800 stations, wandering the train aisles with drinks and snacks for travellers to buy.

PITCH PERFECT

If one thing in India brings everyone together, it's cricket! The country grinds to a halt when a big match is playing, and fans worship their top players as heroes.

⌄ Kolkata's Eden Gardens ground is a venue for Test and One Day International cricket matches.

The Men

India's national
ranks as one of
'The Men in Blue
good at One Day
winning the C
twice and

⌃ Rohit Sharma is a super-high scorer in One Day Internationals.

✓ BACKYARD CRICKET

Indian kids are creative when it comes to cricket, and you'll often see them playing with stumps made from a pile of bricks, crates or even shoes or a stool! If there's no bat, a plank of wood or a stick will do, and the pitch could be a street, beach, back yard or any other open space. There's no official rule book, but that doesn't stop this informal version of the game being a highly competitive sport!

⌄ Anyone of any age can play gally (or gully) cricket.

THE BRITISH INTRODUCED INDIA TO CRICKET IN THE 1700S.

One-day wonders

One of the most-watched tournaments in cricket is the Indian Premier League (IPL) – its sponsorship and TV deals have helped to make India's cricket board the richest in the world. This is a Twenty20 contest, meaning matches are quick with just 20 overs. Eight teams from different Indian cities compete.

≫ When a match is televised, fans will crowd around every available screen.

INDIA OUTDOORS

The UK could fit into India 12 times over! This giant country sweeps from some of the world's highest mountains across plateaus, plains and winding rivers to beaches, islands and swamps.

⌄ Tropical rainforests teem with life in the Andaman Islands of northeast India.

⌃ Kanchenjunga is the third-highest mountain in the world, after Everest and K2 in Nepal.

Mountain highs

The Himalayan mountains tower over northern India, reaching heights of more than 8,000m. Kanchenjunga, the country's tallest peak, is sacred to local people and glints under a cap of snow all year round. Highland plateaus and smaller mountain ranges cover much of southern India too.

Deserts and jungle

India is home to the hot, dry Thar desert (left) as well as some of the wettest places on Earth. In the northeast there are lush tropical rainforests, while the northern Bay of Bengal is fringed with mangrove swamps known as the Sundarbans.

THE VILLAGE OF MAWSYNRAM IN NORTHEAST INDIA IS ONE OF THE WORLD'S RAINIEST INHABITED PLACES!

FOCUS ON

☑ **SEASONAL SOAKING**

India's climate is dominated by the monsoon — a seasonal wind that sweeps across southern Asia. During the hot summer months it blows from the south-west, bringing heavy rains from the Indian Ocean. The first downpour comes in early June and can last for days, with booming thunder and lightning. Then torrential showers come and go between hours of steamy sunshine. The weather starts to dry up in September when the monsoon wind changes direction.

THE GREAT GANGES

One of the world's most famous rivers, the Ganges flows through India from the Himalayas to the Bay of Bengal. More than 500 million people make use of it along its way.

⌃ The river starts from an ice cave under a glacier high in the Himalayas.

River of life

Transport, industry, farming, fishing, washing, drinking… the Ganges supplies water for all these things. Thousands of towns, cities and villages are built along the river, and its delta is one of the most densely populated regions in the world.

⌃ Fishing is an important source of food in the Ganges delta.

⌃ The Ganges is like a washing machine, a bath, a road… and more!

Dirty waters

As the Ganges winds its way past homes, farms and factories, it picks up a lot of pollution (left). Every day, millions of litres of raw sewage and chemicals from industry and farming are dumped in the river. The government is ploughing money into schemes to try to clear it up.

⌄ These workers are taking part in a Ganges cleaning project in Varanasi.

FOCUS ON

☑ HOLY GANGA

For Hindus, the Ganges (right) isn't just a river — it is a goddess too. Millions of pilgrims from all over India come to worship Ganga Ma, or Mother Ganges. In holy cities such as Varanasi, steps called ghats lead down to the river and people flock to bathe and pray. Cremations also happen on the river banks, as scattering ashes on the Ganges is believed to free a person's soul and transport it to heaven.

RURAL INDIA

Living off the land can be really tough, but it's the way many Indians get by. Two-thirds of the population are based in the countryside, and farmers make up half of the nation's workforce.

⌃ Many small farmers keep livestock such as buffaloes or goats.

⌄ The state of Punjab produces so much wheat it is known as the 'breadbasket' of India.

Farm produce

India produces a wide range of crops, including 20 per cent of the world's rice and 12 per cent of its tea. Wheat, maize, sugarcane and cotton also grow well here, especially on the fertile Ganges plain. India is a world leader in milk production, with about 75 million dairy farms – most of these keep buffaloes as opposed to cows!

⌃ Rice planting takes place in a flooded paddy field.

Rural survival

Village life in India is a far cry from the fast-developing towns. Rural people often go without electricity and have to walk to a well for water. Most Indian farmers work on a subsistence level, growing food for their families and selling any extra in local markets. Droughts and floods can cause huge problems, and many country people are very poor.

⚹ Women transport well water on their heads.

MORE THAN 838 MILLION PEOPLE LIVE IN RURAL INDIA – THAT'S OVER TWO-AND-A-HALF TIMES THE POPULATION OF THE WHOLE OF THE USA!

FOCUS ON

☑ FEEDING INDIA

In the 1960s, India launched a 'green revolution' with the aim of boosting farming to feed its growing population. Modern machinery, fertilisers, irrigation and new types of seed all helped to more than double the amount of food produced. Many people think more needs to be done — such as developing high-yield GM (genetically modified) crops. The government is introducing schemes to help farmers, including lending them money and arranging better storage for their harvest.

≫ Machines such as tractors have helped many farmers become more efficient.

WILDLIFE SAFARI

India is known as a megadiverse country, which means it has a mega-rich variety of wildlife and plants. Many of these are protected in national parks and other conservation areas.

Happy snapper

The endangered gharial is a type of crocodile with long, narrow jaws and razor-sharp teeth. The male's snout has a bulge on the end, which creates a strange buzzing sound.

Big eaters

Indian elephants (right) can spend up to 19 hours a day eating! They're sociable animals that migrate in herds to find the best feeding grounds.

Silent stalkers

No two Bengal tigers have the same stripes. Their markings keep them camouflaged while they stalk and ambush their prey.

Rare

Gee's golden langur is one of India's rarest monkeys, found in the foothills of the Himalayas.

FOCUS ON

 BIG BANYAN

Native to India, the banyan tree can grow and grow to cover an enormous area. It sends down shoots from its sprawling branches, which take root and form new trunks. These in turn grow their own branches and roots, spreading the tree even further. The Great Banyan, near Kolkata, is over 250 years old and has more than 3,500 prop or buttress roots — it looks more like a forest than a tree!

Sideways swimmer

The Ganges river dolphin has an interesting habit of swimming on its side, with its flipper trailing in the mud to find food. It is virtually blind and uses echolocation (a way of reflecting sound) to get around.

Hiss

A king cobra can grow to over 5m long and will rear up to look danger in the eye. One bite from this venomous snake is enough to kill an elephant (or 20 humans)!

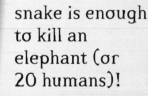

Big bird

India's national bird is the peafowl, the male of which is the colourful peacock. It spends most of its time on the ground but can fly up into trees to roost.

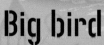

A TOURIST MAGNET

With its exotic scenery and exciting mix of cultures, India has always attracted foreign travellers. About 7 million tourists now arrive every year, mostly from North America and Europe.

⌃ This Jain temple is in the desert town of Jaisalmer.

⌃ Amazing rock-cut monuments fill the Ajanta Caves.

⌄ The Harmandir Sahib is India's holiest Sikh temple.

⌃ The white marble Taj Mahal was built as a tomb.

⌄ The Amber Fort stands near Jaipur.

Golden Triangle

India can be bewildering at first, but there are some well-trodden tourist trails. A typical trip to northern India takes in the 'Golden Triangle' – the cities of Delhi, Agra and Jaipur. In Agra, the Taj Mahal is India's top tourist site, while Jaipur's magic lies in its pink stone buildings.

Beach time

India has a whopping 7,500km of coastline, and golden sandy beaches aren't hard to find. Some of the most popular are in Goa, a state in western India that's known for its relaxed party vibe. India's remote Andaman Islands are a treat for divers and people who want to get away from it all.

⌃ Go to Goa for tropical beaches like this.

FOREIGN TOURISTS SPENT ABOUT $20 BILLION IN INDIA IN 2014.

FOCUS ON

☑ **GOING LOCAL**

Many travellers like to dig deeper into the Indian culture by taking part in a local experience. There are plenty to choose from, whether it's a camel safari in the Thar desert, a cruise on a rice boat in Kerala or a regional cooking course. Local people can make money by getting visitors involved in everyday activities — you can even pay for a day out with Mumbai's dabbawalahs (see p37)!

⌃ Haggling is key if you shop in an Indian market!

« A traditional rice boat ferries tourists through Kerala.

NATURAL ASSETS

Nature provides India with lots of resources, from water to minerals to rainforest timber. But these things are all put under pressure as the population grows.

⌃ The demand for oil from refineries like this is increasing.

Digging deep

India has over 300 billion tonnes of coal reserves and produces about a quarter of the oil it needs. Mines here churn out 88 minerals, including iron ore for the busy steel industry, bauxite for making aluminium, and small amounts of gold and diamonds.

⌄ India depends on coal for about two-thirds of its energy needs.

INDIA RANKS THIRD IN THE WORLD FOR SALT PRODUCTION, EXTRACTING IT FROM BOTH SEAWATER AND ROCKS.

Power plants

Big populations need huge amounts of energy, and India gets most of this from coal-fired power stations. But as people worry more about the environment, renewables such as hydro, solar and wind power are increasing. India is already one of the world's biggest producers of wind power.

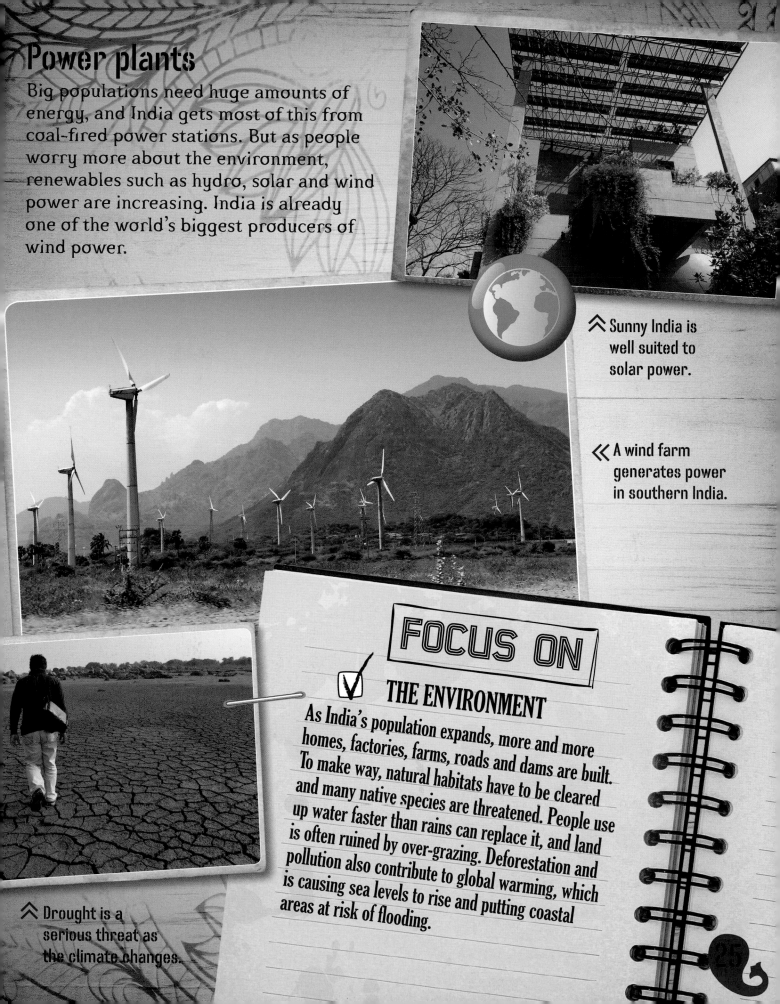

≫ Sunny India is well suited to solar power.

≪ A wind farm generates power in southern India.

≫ Drought is a serious threat as the climate changes.

FOCUS ON

✓ **THE ENVIRONMENT**

As India's population expands, more and more homes, factories, farms, roads and dams are built. To make way, natural habitats have to be cleared and many native species are threatened. People use up water faster than rains can replace it, and land is often ruined by over-grazing. Deforestation and pollution also contribute to global warming, which is causing sea levels to rise and putting coastal areas at risk of flooding.

HIGH-TECH HOTSPOT

ndia has the third-largest pool of scientists in the world, and they have made the country a one-stop-shop for technology. Among other things, India is one of the top five nations for space exploration.

⌄ More than 900 million Indians own a mobile phone.

Computer hubs

India is a global leader in computer software, hardware and other IT services, with millions of young engineers clustered in centres such as Bangalore (India's Silicon Valley), Chennai and Hyderabad. The products they export bring in tens of billions of dollars each year.

⌄ Google is one of many IT companies with offices in Bangalore.

Vehicle manufacture

India's high-tech expertise comes in handy in the automobile industry. The country makes about 17 million vehicles a year, of which 2.3 million are exported. The world's cheapest car, the Tata Nano (right), was launched here in 2009 – and India is also home to Hero, the world's biggest motorbike manufacturer.

INDIANS BOUGHT 200 MILLION MOBILE PHONES IN 2014, AND THE DEMAND KEEPS GROWING!

FOCUS ON

☑ **LOW-TECH**

Many industries in India still battle with time-consuming low-tech systems. Textiles is the country's second-biggest employer after agriculture, but a lack of modern equipment means that productivity is low compared to countries like China. Many people make their living hand-crafting things to sell on the street, or doing manual labour. On small farms (left), it is normal to see an ox or a buffalo pulling a plough, or people harvesting grain by hand.

≫ Many Indian factories lack modern equipment.

GOING GLOBAL

India is making a real impact on the rest of the world. Communities of Indians have spread their culture abroad, and foreigners are rushing to make use of the country's young, skilled workforce.

Work in India

Wages are lower in India than in the West, and that makes the country attractive to foreign businesses. Another benefit is India's enormous English-speaking population. Companies abroad hire Indian firms for their call centres and other services. This is known as outsourcing.

⌃ 'Little India' is an area of Malaysia's capital city, Kuala Lumpur, with a large number of Indian businesses, including restaurants and shops.

⌄ Young people work at an outsourced call centre in Mumbai.

Indians abroad

India's brain drain, where highly qualified people leave to find better-paid jobs, is less of a problem than it was. Many workers are returning to new opportunities in their home country, and bringing global contacts. Indian firms such as Tata (below) are gaining huge success and setting up or buying companies abroad.

FOCUS ON

☑ **MEDICAL TOURISM**

With its high-quality teaching hospitals and research centres, India boasts some of the world's best doctors and surgeons. It also has a thriving pharmaceuticals industry, developing a wide range of medicines. About 250,000 patients travel to India each year for treatments such as hip replacements, cosmetic surgery and heart care. The costs are much lower than in the USA and Europe, but they make India billions of dollars.

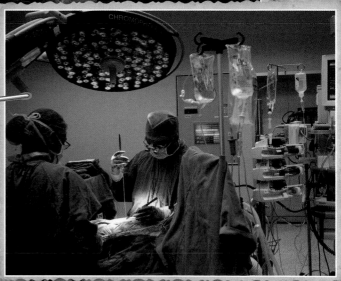

≪ India has many state-of-the-art hospitals where skilled surgeons perform operations.

GROWING UP IN INDIA

Lifestyles in India vary greatly, between cities and the countryside and from rich to poor. But some things are important to everyone, and these include family and tradition.

⌃ Children are often involved in labour, such as collecting or sorting rubbish for recycling.

Close families

Family is at the heart of Indian life, with grandparents, aunts, uncles and cousins all seen as close relatives. They may share a house or live nearby, so there are plenty of people to care for the elderly or the very young. Families consult each other on everything, and many run small businesses together.

⌄ In Indian society, men are traditionally the breadwinners and women often work for less pay.

Going to school

Education in India is free and compulsory for children aged 6-14. While some schools have huge classes and few facilities, others in the private sector are expensive and well-equipped. There are still millions of children in India who don't start school, or leave young to earn money for their families.

>> For rural children, it can be a long walk to school.

∨ Girls now have a better chance at education than they used to.

FOUR WORLD RELIGIONS WERE BORN IN INDIA: HINDUISM, BUDDHISM, SIKHISM AND JAINISM.

∨ Arranged marriages are normal in India, though couples now have more say in the matter. Weddings are often huge and last for days!

FOCUS ON

☑ **FAITH**

There's no official religion in India, but about four in five people are Hindus. Traditionally they are born into a caste, or level of society, and although the system is more relaxed now, people still tend to marry within their caste. Hindus worship many gods and the country is dotted with dazzling temples and shrines. About 13 per cent of Indians are Muslim, and there are also large communities of Christians and Sikhs.

∨ Brihadeeswarar Temple in Thanjavur

31

DATES TO CELEBRATE

The Indian calendar revolves around festivals, usually celebrating religious events or important times in the farming year. They're occasions for bigger crowds and more noise and colour than ever!

Holi

The coming of spring is marked by Holi, another Hindu festival. People celebrate by throwing coloured powder and water at each other out on the streets!

> ⌄ **Getting messy at Holi!**

Diwali

The Hindu New Year kicks off with Diwali, a five-day festival of lights. India glows with candles, lanterns and fireworks to celebrate the victory of good over evil.

> ⌄ **At Diwali, Hindus also engage in rituals such as bathing in the river Ganges.**

Eid-Ul-Fitr

For Muslims, Eid-Ul-Fitr signals the end of Ramadan, a month of fasting. It's a time for feasts, prayers and parties – and a day off work or school!

⌃ Prayer is an important part of Eid.

⌃ A Raksha Bandan friendship bracelet.

Raksha Bandan

For Hindus, Raksha Bandan celebrates the love of brothers and sisters. Siblings tie bracelets around each other's wrists to signify their friendship.

⌃ Sikhs perform a folk dance at the festival of Baisakhi in northern India.

Baisakhi

The biggest festival for Sikhs is Baisakhi, which began as a celebration of harvest and also marks the Sikh New Year.

FOCUS ON

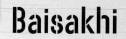

☑ **PUSHKAR CAMEL FAIR**

The most famous festival of Rajasthan, northern India, is the annual Pushkar Camel Fair. It falls in October or November and attracts about 50,000 camels and 200,000 people! Both two- and four-legged revellers dress up and take part in races, games and dance competitions. There's also a fairground and market to enjoy, while many pilgrims come to bathe in the holy waters of Pushkar Lake.

⌃ Camels race at the Pushkar fair.

LOCAL FLAVOURS

Indian food is known for its strong and spicy flavours. Most of the ingredients are home-grown, and many find their way into cooking pots around the world.

⌄ Pick your own spices – if you know what they are!

Spicy sales

An Indian spice market can attack all your senses at once. Big sacks of brightly coloured, aromatic spices are sold by the scoop with everyone haggling for the best price. Among the chilli, ginger, coriander and turmeric there are less familiar flavours such as asafoetida – the dried sap of a tall herb, often used in curry.

⌃ Garam masala is a blend of spices, used as a base in many Indian dishes.

FOCUS ON

☑ TEA

You'll see more tea growing in India than any other country except China! It began on a commercial scale in the days of the East India Company (see p7). The most famous tea-growing regions are Darjeeling and Assam in the north, but there are big plantations in the south of the country too. Tea plants need lots of water, so areas with high rainfall work best. Most of the teas are black teas, though green, white and oolong varieties are becoming increasingly popular.

⌃ Women pick tea leaves in the Darjeeling hills. Darjeeling is known as the 'champagne of teas'.

INDIA CONSUMES MORE THAN 800,000 TONNES OF TEA PER YEAR!

≪ India exports cashews to more than 60 countries.

Feed the world

India is one of the world's biggest producers of fruit and vegetables, with about 44 per cent of all mangoes, 25 per cent of bananas, 35 per cent of onions and a lot more grown there. Many foods are exported, some in processed form such as mango pulp. Rice, nuts and buffalo beef are a few other edibles that India sells abroad.

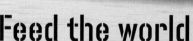

⌃ It's not hard to find your five-a-day here!

TIME TO EAT!

Meals are a time to gather with friends and family, and Indians tend to eat dinner late. It's normal to use your fingers – on your right hand – and scoop up sauces with a flatbread or rice.

⌃ Bread like these chapattis can be used to scoop up food.

Creative curry

India is world-famous for its curries, and they vary enormously from region to region. Most start with onions, garlic, tomatoes, and spices such as ginger, coriander and garam masala. Meat or fish may be added, though many Hindus are vegetarian, none eat beef and Muslims don't eat pork.

⌄ A curry is usually accompanied by rice.

EUROPEANS INVENTED THE WORD 'CURRY', BASED ON THE SOUTH INDIAN KARI – A TYPE OF SAUCE.

Sweet treats

It's amazing what you can do with sugar and condensed milk or ghee (clarified butter)! Indians turn these ingredients into a mouthwatering range of sweets and desserts, adding extras such as fruit or coconut as they go. Mango, pistachio and cardamom are popular flavours for kulfi, a milky Indian ice cream.

⌃ Mixed sweets, or mithai

⌃ Jalebi – deep-fried sweets

⌃ A mango lassi drink

FOCUS ON

☑ TIFFIN

When the British ruled India, they soon discovered that a light meal was best in the heat of the day. It became known as tiffin, and the word stuck! Today tiffin can be anything from a packed lunch to a street snack or afternoon tea. In Mumbai, a busy network of dabbawalas ('box carriers') have made it their business to deliver freshly cooked food from people's homes to their offices. They transport colour-coded lunchboxes (below) to more than 300,000 workers every day!

THE BIG SCREEN

Welcome to Bollywood, the biggest movie industry in the world! Based in Mumbai, it churns out more films than Hollywood and rakes in hundreds of millions of dollars a year.

⌃ Extras on the set of a Bollywood movie pose for a photo.

Bollywood style

Feel-good films with catchy song-and-dance numbers are what makes Bollywood such a hit. Plots tend to follow a 'boy meets girl' theme, with various mishaps along the way. There's action, humour and plenty of glamour – glitzy costumes and attractive stars are key.

≫ Bollywood dance is energetic and flamboyant.

THE BIGGEST-EVER BOLLYWOOD DANCE INVOLVED 4,428 PEOPLE!

38

Bollywood big-time

Salman Khan and Shah Rukh Khan are arch rivals turned friends who tussle for the top spot on the Bollywood star rich list. Amitabh Bachchan is up there too, and the most followed Indian celebrity on Twitter.

⌃ Street musicians play traditional instruments, including a drum and a tanpura.

⌃ Bollywood stars Shah Rukh Kahn (left) and Deepika Padukone attend a film premiere.

Song and dance

Indian dances often tell a story, with hand gestures and facial expressions meaning different things. They might be accompanied by Indian classical music, which is made up of layers – the melody (raag), rhythm (tal), and a long drone note played on a string instrument called the tanpura.

FOCUS ON

☑ **MOVIE BOOM**

Bollywood films are made mainly in the Hindi language, and sometimes in English or Hinglish (a blend of the two!). This means that they're popular across the country, but other parts of India have huge film industries too. Tollywood, Mollywood, Chhollywood, Kollywood… they all exist! Each one is produced in a local language and collects bumper ticket sales. Multiplex cinemas are springing up everywhere as people's incomes are growing and they have more leisure time.

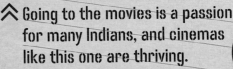

⌃ Going to the movies is a passion for many Indians, and cinemas like this one are thriving.

PLAY TIME

Despite the Indians' passion for cricket (see p12-13), hockey is the national sport. Wrestling, football and basketball are popular too, and many other activities have their origins here.

⌃ Chess stems from the ancient Indian game Chaturanga.

Indian games

India was the birthplace of snakes and ladders, ludo and the original form of chess! Card games, using painted rags, were played in ancient India too. Kabaddi, a popular type of contact sport, was also invented here – not surprisingly, India has the most successful world team.

≫ Kabaddi is played in two teams of seven, with 'raiders' taking turns to tag players on the opposite side.

≫ Snakes and ladders began in ancient India, as a way of teaching morals to children.

Yoga

When it comes to mind and body health, yoga is a popular pastime – and fans of it can thank the Indians! The word yoga comes from the ancient Indian Sanskrit language and was mentioned in old sacred texts. Many people go on yoga retreats to India for a relaxing, feel-good holiday.

≪ Yoga is a spiritual experience as well as a physical activity.

IN 2015, 35,985 PEOPLE LIMBERED UP AT THE WORLD'S LARGEST YOGA LESSON IN NEW DELHI!

≫ A flying Bengal tiger roars through the air at the International Kite Festival of Gujarat.

FOCUS ON

☑ HIGH FLIERS

Every January, the Indian state of Gujarat hosts a gigantic kite festival. Kite-flying is popular in India, and it's taken very seriously. Leading up to the festival, people spend months making brightly coloured kites out of paper and bamboo. Then they gather on rooftops to fly them. Fighter kites, called patangs, have a string coated in glue and ground glass, which becomes very sharp when it dries. The aim of kite fighting is to cut every other kite out of the sky.

COLOURFUL AND CREATIVE

Indians have had more than 5,000 years to perfect their arts and crafts! Ancient texts talk about pottery, weaving, woodcrafting and other skills that are still in play today.

Lucky Rangoli

If you visit an Indian house on a special occasion, you might be greeted by a Rangoli. This is a decorative pattern made on the floor or walls, usually with coloured rice, flour, sand or chalk. Traditionally the shapes are based on nature, such as leaves, flowers or birds. Rangoli are thought to bring good luck.

⌃ An Indian craftswoman paints colourful designs onto fabric.

SOME INDIAN ARTISTS PAINT WITH NATURAL PIGMENTS, INCLUDING THE SPICE TURMERIC, RICE POWDER AND SOOT.

« Coloured rice was carefully laid on the floor to produce this Rangoli peacock.

Miniature painting

Painting enormous detail into tiny pictures takes a steady hand and excellent eyesight! Indian miniature art came to the fore during Mughal times, using paints made with pure gold or precious stones for dazzling colours. Artists in India still train in miniature painting today.

>> A grand procession becomes minuscule in this pocket-sized Indian painting!

FOCUS ON

☑ **DECORATIVE DRESS**

Everyday dress in India can look like a masterpiece in itself. Clothes are often beautifully embroidered or printed with eye-catching patterns. A typical woman's outfit is the sari — a long strip of colourful fabric that's carefully draped around the body. This might be accompanied by golden jewellery and a dot of colour on the forehead called a bindi. Mehndi is the Indian art of painting hands and feet with fancy henna tattoos.

≪ This woman has mehndi painted on her hands for a festival.

43

ALL EYES ON INDIA

India is the world's biggest democracy and its economy is growing fast. Yet the country still has many problems and millions of people struggle to survive. How do things look for the future?

⌃ Shopping centres like this one in Delhi are an attraction for India's growing middle classes.

Mixed wealth

The middle class in India is expanding, with more and more people enjoying modern homes, cars, gadgets and money to spend. But not everyone is benefiting from new, well-paid jobs – about one in four Indians still live in poverty, making up around a third of the world's poor.

⌃ More than 800 million Indians are eligible to vote. Electronic voting machines make the process easier.

People pressure

India crams a population almost as big as China's into a third of the area. This puts a lot of pressure on its resources and economy. Finding housing, jobs, healthcare and education for everyone is a challenge for the future, as is producing enough food and energy to go round.

⌄ Construction workers like these often struggle on very low pay.

INDIA HAS 90 BILLIONAIRES, WHILE HUNDREDS OF MILLIONS OF PEOPLE LIVE ON LESS THAN $2 A DAY.

⌃ By 2030, India's population is predicted to be over 1.5 billion.

FOCUS ON

☑ **WORLD RELATIONS**

Like most countries, India relies on other nations for its survival. For example, importing oil and other goods helps to back up its own resources, and exporting things like crops, minerals and vehicles brings in significant money. The government recently launched a 'Make in India' initiative to encourage foreign companies to manufacture their products here. The hope is to attract investment and create jobs, increase skills and improve lives for many Indians.

QUIZ

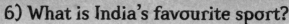

How much do you know about India's land and people? Try this quick quiz and find out!

1) What is the capital of India?
a) Mumbai
b) Kolkata
c) New Delhi

2) What is the Indian currency?
a) Ruble
b) Rupee
c) Yen

3) Which mountains tower over northern India?
a) The Himalayas
b) The Andes
c) The Alps

4) What was the Taj Mahal built as?
a) A palace
b) A tomb
c) A fort

5) Which of these musical instruments comes from India?
a) Maracas
b) Bagpipes
c) Tanpura

6) What is India's favourite sport?
a) Cricket
b) Baseball
c) Basketball

7) What would you do with a chapatti?
a) Wear it
b) Drive it
c) Eat it

8) Are the majority of Indians…?
a) Hindu
b) Muslim
c) Buddhist

9) Which of these Indian creatures is venomous?
a) Bengal tiger
b) King cobra
c) Indian elephant

10) What is garam masala?
a) A type of tea
b) A Bollywood dance
c) A blend of spices

11) Ancient Indian civilisation began in the valley of which river?
a) The Ganges
b) The Indus
c) The Brahmaputra

12) What is kabaddi?
a) A sport
b) A curry
c) A festival

True or false?
1) More Indians live in cities than the countryside.
2) India has more English speakers than the USA.
3) The word shampoo comes from India.

Answers: 1c, 2b, 3a, 4b, 5c, 6a, 7c, 8a, 9b, 10c, 11b, 12a True or false? 1F, 2F, 3T

GLOSSARY

autorickshaw
A small, motorised, three-wheeled vehicle used like a taxi.

camouflaged
Blending in with particular surroundings.

chai
The name for tea in India.

commuter
Someone who travels to work.

deforestation
Clearing an area of forest or trees.

delta
An area of low-lying coastal land, built up by sediment from a river.

democracy
A country that is governed by elected leaders.

export
To send goods or services to another country for sale.

GM crops
Crops that have been genetically modified in a way that doesn't occur naturally.

irrigation
Supplying water to help crops grow.

mangrove
A tree or shrub that grows in swamps around the coast and survives in salty water at high tide.

megacity
A city of over 10 million people.

migrant
A person who moves from one place to another to live.

monsoon
A seasonal wind that affects southern Asia, blowing in different directions at different times of year.

One Day International
A form of cricket where each team faces a set number of overs and the match is usually completed in a day.

peninsula
A piece of land projecting into the sea or another body of water.

pilgrim
Someone who travels to a sacred place for religious reasons.

plateau
An area of fairly level high ground.

rural
Relating to the countryside as opposed to towns.

sacred
Of religious importance, such as being linked with a god or goddess.

sugarcane
A tropical grass with a tall, wide stem from which sugar can be extracted.

urban
Relating to towns or cities.

venomous
Capable of ejecting venom (poison) by biting or stinging.

Further information

Books

India by Darryl Humble (Franklin Watts, 2013)

Unpacked: India by Susie Brooks (Wayland, 2013)

Developing World: Delhi and Mumbai by Jenny Vaughan (Franklin Watts, 2016)

Discover Countries: India by Tim Atkinson (Wayland, 2012)

Journey Along a River: The Ganges by Paul Harrison (Wayland, 2013)

Radar: Bhangra and Bollywood by Anna Claybourne (Wayland, 2011)

20th Century Lives: Bollywood Stars by Liz Gogerly (Wayland, 2010)

Websites

www.roughguides.com/destinations/asia/india
A travel guide to India.

www.tajmahal.org.uk
All about the Taj Mahal.

http://india.gov.in/india-glance
Country information from the Indian government.

http://www.bbc.co.uk/schools/primaryhistory/indus_valley/land_of_the_indus/
A visit to ancient India.

Index